When Flowers Bloom and Fall

A collection of poems

Bismay Mohanty

Copyright © 2025 Bismay Mohanty

All Rights Reserved.

This book has been self-published with all reasonable efforts taken to make the material error-free by the author. No part of this book shall be used, reproduced in any manner whatsoever without written permission from the author, except in the case of brief quotations embodied in critical articles and reviews.

The Author of this book is solely responsible and liable for its content including but not limited to the views, representations, descriptions, statements, information, opinions and references ["Content"]. The Content of this book shall not constitute or be construed or deemed to reflect the opinion or expression of the Publisher or Editor. Neither the Publisher nor Editor endorse or approve the Content of this book or guarantee the reliability, accuracy or completeness of the Content published herein and do not make any representations or warranties of any kind, express or implied, including but not limited to the implied warranties of merchantability, fitness for a particular purpose. The Publisher and Editor shall not be liable whatsoever for any errors, omissions, whether such errors or omissions result from negligence, accident, or any other cause or claims for loss or damages of any kind, including without limitation, indirect or consequential loss or damage arising out of use, inability to use, or about the reliability, accuracy or sufficiency of the information contained in this book.

Made with ❤ on the Notion Press Platform

www.notionpress.com

For the souls who know

that every bloom is sacred,

every fall – holy,

and love, in all its forms,

is the most beautiful becoming.

Contents

Preface

I had thought to name this collection of poems "From Heavens to Heartbreaks" for a long period of time. If you carefully observe the cover then you may find that title more apt to this. However, the inclusion of a negative word made me feel that readers might judge the book by its cover! So just before sending this book to publication, the renaming was done to "When Flowers Bloom and Fall" – depicting that everything that once joyfully starts eventually fades with the passage of time.

Life cannot exist without death preceding it, just as positive and negative charges coexist within an atom. Every ending mark the beginning of something new. Everything is intertwined through logical and inexplicable patterns in this vast and mysterious universe. Just as light and shadow, joy and sorrow coexist, so too do heaven and heartbreak.

You might wonder—how can heartbreak be the opposite of heaven? When someone is in love, that emotion seeps into every corner of their life—into their prayers, their dreams, their ambitions, even their silences. Love makes everything feel divine. But when that love shatters, the world may seem to collapse. Yet, that collapse doesn't mean it's the end.

How can it be hell when there are still kind souls who help you heal? When nature still breathes its calm into your chaos, through its breeze, its rain, its quiet embrace? Even amidst a mental storm, we continue to function, to smile, to survive. It isn't hell. It's just heartbreak—a passing phase that eventually fades.

We often find comfort in revisiting beautiful memories, but rarely muster the strength to confront the painful ones that once broke us. With this collection of poems, I hope to offer you space for both the delight and the discomfort, the rise and the fall. Because both are parts of the same passion. Both deserve to be heard.

Thank you for choosing to read this book. I hope it resonates with you, and I'd love to hear your thoughts as you journey through it.

Bismay Mohanty

20th May, 2025

Acknowledgments

This book would not have been possible without the love, support, and encouragement of many people who have stood by me throughout my journey.

I am deeply grateful to my grandfather, Bhupen Dasmahapatra, an eminent Odia author, whose literary legacy and wisdom have always been a guiding light in my life. His influence has shaped my passion for writing in more ways than words can express.

My heartfelt thanks to Ashutosh Acharya, columnist at The Indian Express, for his thoughtful guidance and belief in my work. Your encouragement has meant a great deal to me.

To Kiran Sourav Das, my ever-ready reader—thank you for always being the first to read, respond, and resonate with my words. Your support has kept my creative spirit alive.

I would like to thank my sister-in-law, Sushmita Das, for designing the beautiful cover of this book. Your creative vision gave a face to my words, and I'm truly grateful for your effort and care.

To my brother, Biplab, thank you for constantly reminding me to follow what brings me joy. Your quiet strength and support have always been a source of comfort.

To my parents and elders—thank you for your blessings and belief in me. Your love and values are the foundation of everything I do.

A special thanks to my former colleagues in Bangalore – Pruthvi, Mahima, Akhil Shaw, Anto, Akhil Vyas, Vaseef, Dinesh, Ravindra, Anand, and Thendral. Your support, regardless of our career paths, has truly meant the world to me.

I am also fortunate to be part of my current organization, which has been incredibly supportive and encouraging of my creative pursuits. I am grateful to be in a space that values personal passions alongside professional growth.

Lastly, to all the beautiful souls who still seek poetry as a form of reflection, healing, and hope thank you. Your love for words and meaning reminds me why I write. This book is for you.

when flowers bloom

1. Dreamland

Floating on a mist of love embracing the skin

In a home from which far I had been

My eyes are closed and yet I see all

Travelers celebrating after death in the yawl.

There is a world far away from here

Where anything you do, people cheer

No boundaries anywhere as we can read hearts

Of each other, and without saying convo starts.

It's a land of dreamers – Dreamland it is called

Where love doesn't need poetries or words scrawled

We, dreamers, connect through music within

As shown in movies the union of two souls begins.

Here, in Dreamland only those are allowed who dream

Anything is fine, but dreaming is a must, with or without a theme

A kind of home where I always wanted to be at

Something which mortal life prohibits from building or making that.

Monday morning, and back to Reality

The compelling need for survival is back in all totality

The next tour to Dreamland is again five days far away;

Till then I should work on those tickets by Friday.

2. A Desire

There is an immense desire in me

To rest my head on the warmth of your lap

Looking at your lips, tracing the path your eyes follow

As you read me a book in the evenings after sunset

Your hair brushing the shoulder

And spreading all across the book

By the gush of wind from the open window

My fingers shall run your hairs back

And place them behind the ear.

A mid sentence drop in the reading comes

Like the chapter has come to an end

Then I see your eyes tracing lines no more

They are diving into mine deep and whole

The smile on your lips reflects some gloss

From the dim table lamp in the corner.

Next desire would be to turn it off

When stories shall end from the book

Together we will gaze at the stars -

The halogen ones stuck on the ceiling

Holding hands, laying on the bed.

Can you please read some pages

From the book of your life?

The immense desire in me longs

To be a character in your story

Why not a protagonist?

Because nobody can steal your role from you

These desires are something dynamic

Once they were to be accepted

Slowly drifting to beg your love

Needs then grow to be a part of your life

I thank you to open the doors for me

I was a happy onlooker at the street

Quenching my eyes looking up to you

Standing at the roof and smiling from above

Like from paradise, an angel has come

The desire is to stay with you ever since.

3. Long distance relationship

When I walk down the aisle of memories

Encountering a path of dropped thorns and blooming leaves

Questions that collided within the neurons

Imagining answers in a frenzy that never stops

But today is a normal day, and it's been such for a long time

Where every moment we share on its own becomes a soothing rhyme

The hallucination of waking next to you each time I sleep

And finding you on my phone is a reality to acknowledge deep

Exchanges of morning wishes, sharing plans for the day at breakfast

A joyous smile spreads across the face, for a great time it does last

Till we meet again in the cacophonies of dusk over tea

Our lands are so similar yet distant, as if cut off by the sea

Reaching out to each other is a matter of patience

For the power of love spells magic to remove all the distance

And we read books to each other after sunset

Over voice notes make us feel so close, I don't regret

While I have my dinner tonight listenin tog you on the call

Uncooked tortilla dipped in watery pulses is not an issue at all

Descending into my dreams, as I kiss you goodnight

A little closer to your arms, I feel tonight.

4. No ghosts anymore

Darkness all around in the room

Creaking doors and fear of ghosts

That you are afraid of so many things at once

Nothing to worry about, dear, don't feel low.

Look out of the window at the clear sky

I have begged the moon to be there for you

Since she, too, glows despite being all black

No quality is less than the moon you lack.

Now that you feel guarded from above

Smile a bit and go to bed; you look beautiful

The ghosts have escaped your boundary

Shielded by the spell of divine armory.

As you lay your head on the pillow,

And peacefully shut your eyelids close

Did you feel that kiss on the side of your forehead?

No ghosts anymore from now, for my eyes have read.

5. Scorching Sun

Moon looked at me and smiled

She will convey my poems compiled

To the one awaiting – a one in a billion.

An oblivion of ecstasy as sleep came to the eyes

Hovering on top of me were some fireflies

Places to travel with love, no other intention.

Dreams of us in fields, mountains, and beaches

Some love to learn and some to teach

Endless energy to rest, endless again to run.

The evening was spent on the roof, and so was all night

Dawn calls for reality, waking up with all might

For survival, some time to pause the passion.

Now that I am out of my home

Can't dream of you at the office, I'll meet you alone

Every mirror holds your smile in reflection.

Home again and on the roof – the chest is bare

My heart filled with despair

Will you love me like the scorching sun?

6. So, Let's Go

Why do we seek rain when the sun is out?

Why do we seek sun when the rain is there?

Till when life shall get about all wishing

And dreaming all the possible things

Which could be lived totally?

So let's go

To every place the roads can lead.

Maybe we will listen to all the songs

On our Spotify playlist.

So let's go

Every temple where we dream't to be

Beyond sky and all infinity.

7. Voice and Silence

I know not of the hearing impaired

Whether the silence is a blessing

Or they helplessly cry for endurance

For me, it's a different guilt altogether

When a day goes without your voice

As my mornings battle the quiet

Which is too loud to wake up

And in the grave stillness, my days go

Unnoticed, uncalled, and all unknown.

Beloved,

I meet loneliness in every place

Where a dint of void you cannot see

That's all the courage to sleep with lights off

Emptiness everywhere indeed it is

WHEN FLOWERS BLOOM AND FALL

The urge to listen to music is all gone

Every song reminds me of you

And how bad an escapism it is

Trying to sleep in the afternoon

To rush through the unending time

Volcano of tears escapes the crater of my eyes

The haunting silence still awaits me

Evening feels like the world has ended

The only sign of life I find

It's when I receive your phone call

Sometimes I go through the recordings

That blesses all my existence

Thanking God for not throwing me

Into the era of letters and postcards

As such then in every way

I would prefer to be hearing-impaired.

8. Sunrise Without You

The morning glories do not come

And it doesn't hurt, for I have got accustomed.

With all enthusiasm when the day starts

Your absence everywhere makes me fall apart.

From my bedsheets and your hair on the pillow

Whenever I wake up to your hello

Can you be there when I open my eyes?

Your presence would have been a paradise.

When I start my day with the food

Has a touch of your hands in it

Tea stalls have lost their charm too

I only love it when I am with you.

Thus, with a hundred thoughts, I get up from bed

With your absence, it is as good as dead

Awaiting eagerly for that infinite new

When no longer shall I have any sunrise without you.

9. As I Pray for You

When I pray for you in silence deep,

A smile stirs where shadows sleep.

I close my eyes, and there you are

A gentle light, my guiding star.

Your smiling face begins to shine,

And in that glow, your soul meets mine.

No words exchanged, yet hearts converse,

In the prayerful pause, the universe.

A smile blooms upon my face

A mirrored joy, your silent grace.

As if your soul just whispered near,

And wiped away my every fear.

Like flowers kissed by morning dew,

I feel alive just thinking of you.

Yet I won't pluck this sacred bloom,

Nor rush to fill the silent room.

For love is not a cage or a chain,

Nor something built from spoken strain.

A flower lives its truest truth,

On the branch of tender youth.

So let me love you from afar,

As skies still love the evening star.

No need to speak or rearrange,

For love is pure, and need not change.

I won't confess to twist your fate,

Or plant a seed that blooms too late.

I'll guard this feeling, wild and free,

Like rivers that flow endlessly.

When I pray for you, you're close—so near,
Your presence whispers, soft and clear.

And if you smile – just once, somewhere,

Know that my heart was already there.

10. Declaration

Thunderstorms laugh with me

Clouds burst as per their density

When purpose is defined by destiny

Fate no longer remains an enemy.

The winds may roar, but I stand still,

With fire in heart and unshaken will.

Each scar I wear like royalty's crest,

Proof that I gave life my very best.

Mountains bend when the soul is free,

Even shadows bow to tenacity.

I rise not for glory or fame,

But to honor love in Bismay's name.

Let trials come, let tempests scream,

I walk awake inside my dream.

No storm, no loss can silence me –

For I am carved in poetry.

11. Flowers

I want to be the reason why flowers bloom

Even if I cannot keep them that way forever

Though flowers have lovers of all sorts

Some pray for rain and await the buds to grow

Some come every day to pluck for their gods.

But there is the thing about flowers:

They don't know why the gardener made efforts for them.

To sell them off for the dead or idol garlands

Or if he wanted them to flourish freely and be safe in a home.

Humans in love are plucked to offer their soulmates

While nature lovers let them stay in their homes

It's not love if I pluck her to keep her in my room, decorated in a glass jar

You will know it's love when I see her cheerful and living - from far.

12. My Name Is Love

I was born in the hush before thunder,

A whisper in the storm's strong chest

Not made of silk, but of something tougher,

Like fire wrapped in tenderness.

I walk not in shadows, but beside them,

Holding hands with the ones who fall.

I am not the echo of fleeting passion

I am the one who answers the call.

I carry the weight of your silence,

Like a knight bears the oath on his sword.

I speak not just in words, but in presence,

In the way I wait without reward.

I am not perfect; I've bled from battles

Where hearts were castles set aflame.

But still I come, again, unshaken

Each wound a prayer, each scar a name.

I know the language of breaking,

Of tears disguised in grins.

I know when to be still and hold you

As the war within you spins.

I burn, but not to consume you,

Only to light your path through night.

I do not seek to change your wings,

Only to keep them in my sight.

I am not here to bind or burden,

But to honor the steps you take.

Even when the world grows colder,

I'll be warmth you didn't have to make.

My name is Love, not because I own you,

But because I see you through and through.

I am man enough to fight with silence

And soft enough to kneel with you.

So come when you're weary, or wild, or wrong

This road we take, we'll rise above.

No map, no guide, no vow too strong,

Just me. Just you. My name is Love.

13. The Muse of My Poems

I wrote emotions on pages,

Wove dreams into every line.

Dressed love in English verses,

As if they were a secret path to your shrine.

I slipped your name quietly into every rhyme,

Painted your smile, your walk, your every sign.

"She is the moonlight of my darkest night,"

I wrote, hoping to make your soul align.

I poured my heart in rhythmic emotion,

Lived on the hope of your silent devotion.

Each stanza longed to whisper your name,

Each verse was a candle in your flame.

At times, I wrote – hello

"Her silence is a thousand suns setting on my
soul..."

Or

"Her absence is a poem that never becomes whole."

I believed you'd read and finally know,

That in my world, you are the glow.

But one day you said

"I don't understand your English poems..."

And my universe collapsed in slow motion.

I thought you'd be the muse of my poetic sea,

Finding pieces of yourself in each melody.

But you were just quiet, lost in apathy,

Neither grasping the rhyme, nor the symphony.

That day I learned

Love isn't built just in rhyme,

You have to speak the language

Of the one you want to make yours in time.

Now I wonder,

Instead of poetry, I should have looked into your
eyes and simply said

"I love you, deeply and endlessly."

14. And Yet…

I was never good with spoken words,

They always failed me,

Fell apart on my tongue,

Like paper boats in a stormy sea.

I've always found solace in writing,

Because there, I am unfiltered and real.

People say, "Just say it out loud,"

But I only know how to bleed through a pen,

Not through speech I can't feel.

I hoped my poems would confess it all,

You'd read them and hear the echo of my pain,

My quiet waiting, my fading flame…

But when you said, "I don't get it,"

It was the first time even my words felt vain.

Now I'm torn…

Should I speak, or should I hide?

But maybe… maybe I'll keep these feelings inside.

Because I'd rather let them remain unheard

Than break my heart into grains of dust,

Scattered by the winds,

Never to be gathered or touched.

I'll tuck them away

Like unfinished poems,

Like unsaid prayers.

Because I was never made to shout my love.

And I don't want you to see me

In a thousand shattered pieces,

Too small to ever become whole again.

The muse of my poems

You never became.

But my poems…

They still whisper your name.

15. Whispers of Rain

The clouds had sulked in shades of grey,

Yet I sped ahead, I didn't stay.

The sky wept softly on my face,

A gentle hush, a wild embrace.

The wheels beneath hummed songs of flight,

Through winds that danced with pure delight.

Each raindrop kissed my open skin,

Like mother's hands had once been in

The evening bath of yesteryears,

With warmth in touch and eyes of tears.

Adolescence burns with sweet unrest,

A rebel heart inside my chest.

I know the road, I know the gate,

Where home still stands in patient wait.

But rain has ways to make me roam,

To taste the world and still feel home.

There's love, perhaps, that isn't real

Yet in this breeze, her silence feels.

She rides with me in phantom light,

In laughter hushed, in shadows bright.

Her fingers wrap around my soul,

She fills the spaces time can't hold.

The storm recedes, the clouds pull wide,

And I – with freedom as my guide

Still ride through drops that fall like grace,

With her in dreams, wind on my face.

No map, no end, no reason why

Just me, the rain, the open sky.

16. I Wish You Forever

I wish you forever like sun to the sky,

Not bound by hours that drift or die,

But ever-burning, calm or clever,

A timeless flame I wish you forever.

I wish you laughter that bursts like spring,

In gardens where joy learns to sing,

Each petal of peace, each drop of cheer,

May bloom in your soul year after year.

I wish you mornings soft as prayer,

With golden light woven through air,

And nights that hold your dreams like pearls

Safe from the noise of fleeting worlds.

I wish you strength not forged in stone,

But grown where kindest hearts are sown,

The kind that bends but never breaks,

That holds the world for others' sakes.

I wish you love not just romance,

But the kind that lifts with every glance,

The love that sees, the love that stays,

In quiet hours and crowded days.

I wish you hope that never tires,

A soul that sings, a heart that fires,

A dance through storms, a fearless stride

With purpose burning bright inside.

And more than all, this sacred tether:

May life and light be yours together.

To one whose spirit soars and gives

I wish you forever, as long as it lives.

17. World of Love

The word that I love you

Has spread all over the wind

And it follows me wherever I go

Someone might have surreptitiously witnessed

Both of us together in the murky of the night

Someone might have eavesdropped

While we were bound by passion

That someone who originated the whispers

That is spreading like a wildfire by now

Assuring it was us and nobody else there

Hence the sound of the trumpets is far and wide

But that night we were all alone

I remember

There were no people, also there were no trees

Neither were there any birds, nor flora, fauna, or
insects

Then who was this mysterious uncanny person

In the proximity of whose we were sitting

Does the lake recognize you, dear beloved?

When we hid from the entire world

And made ourselves all alone

Selflessly uniting the hearts of each other

Tying the knots of beliefs with time

I assure you it is safe and secured

When our teary eyes gave got a new life

Briefly, as we conversed silently

It might be some notorious dust that blew with the
wind

Got to know of us and everything in our hearts,

Some dust from the wind

Or some stars from the sky

Have committed this sin

Either of these two is the culprit

I know for sure

But don't you worry, dear beloved!

Come, let's walk together

And build a different world

Where none but us would be there

And we both alone would be there.

18. The Killers of Love

As silence echoes in the core of the soul

A dead, cold stiffening of blood and art

When our existence is limited

But expectations infinite

Aren't we a baggage of conditions

Waiting for unconditional love?

There are eight billion people on Earth

Our paths cross with only a few hundred

Even fewer than a dozen care,

Apart from the picture, there is nothing to share.

There might be a plethora of pictures

None are substantial enough to remind you of anything

A hollow blank memory lived, and is gone

The album for the future needs to change

Whatever doesn't impact must be thrown

Again, let's not live by the pictures

Tell me your story, tell me your goals

Tell me all, let's not be strangers anymore

We will become children once again

With innocence pure -

Counting a sky full of stars

Playing without a wristwatch

Seeing sunrises and sunsets

Learning to live and learning to love

Unlike the idea of mature people who say

"I love chicken", so you kill what you love.

19. You are Mine

Living in a world

Where everything without you

At all, doesn't seem fine

Let's reside in a world

In close proximity will be you and I

How long for this togetherness shall we keep trying?

No matter where you were

Where you are and where you will be

The truth shall remain that you are mine.

Under drizzling rain with a tinge of sunshine

Our fingers entwine

When without you days lived and breathes taken

Make me count of time

Darling, shall you make your world

Within the perimeter of my arms?

20. Expressing Love

When I express you love, my love

It's not out of any guilt or fever

Every time I make you sad, a thought comes

Of your crying face that makes me quiver.

In the swaying of green leaves

When maple leaves fall and breezes stay

Likewise, our love shall remain

And tensions drop to be stray.

And whenever the breeze comes again

We shall fly together like dandelions

Awaiting a human birth to grow, educate and wait

When I put on your forehead, a pinch of vermilion.

21. Awaiting a union

I desire to quench this summer thirst

Of engulfing you in my arms and embrace

Just like I came across you once

May we meet soon too by God's grace.

Two states are not really that far

Boundaries are nothing but lines drawn

So close we are living in the one country

One continent, one planet and so on.

Your cotton candy lips are melting in my mouth

I can imagine it all clear and loud

Nevertheless, when I go searching for you

You shall cherish each moment as I am found.

BISMAY MOHANTY

And fall

22. Illusion

I wanted nothing but to catch the sun.

Sometimes it hid, blushing behind the window of leaves.

Sometimes behind the curtain of clouds.

Whenever I chased, it was ensured to rest well as speed doesn't confirm my liveliness when I meet it.

Still in my stillness, I could only wave goodbyes,

Even when sunset comes and my waiting gets prolonged through a winter night

I can only catch it the next day, this time not chasing but by extending my hand

Whose touch gets untouched

As I close my palm and imagine holding it

But it's too far away...

23. Maya

Once upon a time,

A random person spat on the Buddha.

Buddha showed no reaction

Rather calmed his angry disciple even

And thanked the man who spat, said

"Please come and spit whenever you feel like".

Maya came to my life similarly

Smiling and blushing and acting

First, she took all that was needed

To win a trust that she loves me.

Next moment, I was crying over a toy

That was supposed be the world for me

And I made the mistake of sharing it.

Once and again,

Maya comes in front

When life goes all smooth

And I write another poetry like this one

That everyone except her read

Because she is busy in her duty

Of testing people who are delicate.

The Buddha was yet to come out of me

I was sitting at a vegan restaurant today

As I had my cap on and also my hoodie

Peeped a bit to see Maya in the view

And she constantly looked back

It was me who was there – a youth in love.

She did her usual acting of liking him then.

I got up from my seat calmly and left

It wasn't much that I cared for Maya

Her smile never faded from my memory

But I cared for the guy who was there

He would be watching the stars and smiling

Or might be writing poems during study hours

Doing everything that he is going to regret later.

24. Often I Think You're Better Without Me

Often I think you're better without me,

A bird that's soaring high, forever free.

You push me away though I long to stay near,

While I chase your shadow, you disappear.

I watch as you stand in your world, so bright,

A star in the distance, lost to my sight.

I reach for your hand, but you pull it away,

As if my presence might lead you astray.

Am I the storm that you fear will arrive?

Or am I the calm in which you can't survive?

Each step I take closer, you slip out of reach,

Like waves pulling back from a forgotten beach.

Perhaps you're lighter when I'm not around,

No ties to the earth, no feet on the ground.

But still, in my heart, I ache to belong,

Even when silence feels louder than song.

Yet even as walls between us arise,

I'll keep searching for love in your eyes.

For though you push me, I'll never be free,

Of wanting you closer, as close as can be.

25. Insignificant

Propelling the prayers of hours for several days

In the disruptions of sinew making worth it every pain

That's called being a man

Profound synchronicities not planted

Discovered at every step on the way

God laid a path to walk on, we have to pay

Though in front there is comfort zone and wisdom

Logic drowns to self and dreams of being immortal

And what of us for whom you had these dreams in total?

Took weeks to grow dandelions

You ransacked them all as I let you dance on my garden

I only went to click yours, a facade welcomed me then

There is no point of having friendships at this stage

With the like-minded, those guys are depressed as hell

Dopamine, alcohol, drugs, parties – their fairy tale

Reach out to the stars and name a Milky Way on someone

You won't be in their thoughts, their art, their dream

Abstract foolery by efforts, reincarnation awaits to redeem.

26. The Eerie Silence of Every Night

When the cook drops the huge tiffin

On the table in front of my room

I wake up with the sound

Like an alarm that calls to get up

To avoid the loss of food.

As I go to the office, I take my steps

There are no headphones on my ears

Maybe they want to catch something

As simple as the gardener watering the plants

Footsteps rustling on the sidewalk.

Headphones are on everyone's head around me

Once I enter the building, cutting all serenity

When the motivation drops, then

And emerges a true existential crisis

The mind is tricked by looking at your pictures

An angel's company is the reward for surviving the day.

The hours clock by immersed in work

Even if the eyes hurt and the head aches

I long to get a glimpse of my angel, but in vain

As all good things take time

Awaiting you to come online is one such event, too.

The room is in darkness, and all this time

Just like my life and my day

As soon as your voice shakes the wind chime

Lights turn on and welcome a bright smile

Here arrives the best of the day – rewarding.

The laughter and the love

Songs, meditation, and talks

Fill up the purpose of all

Like a reader's happiness over a writer's struggle

The books end when my angel has to depart

Thereby welcoming the eerie silence of every night.

27. Disinterested

When the tight cheeks pulled by others are a distant memory of irritation

Has now turned into soggy layers of wrinkles with nobody to touch

The insomnia reflects under the eyes

And belly fat denotes disinterest in life

There was a time after a hectic school day when the energy burst to get back home

No excitement now for returning to a place after work, where even ghosts won't haunt

Once, there was sadness when people left

Now there's none as if humans are ringing the wind chime

With so many changes inside and out, I find a stranger in the mirror

Was it never me who lived once, or is the present me trying to live?

28. Fading

If suddenly tomorrow,

You don't get to see me,

Like a shadow fading softly,

Into the morning sea.

If the winds no longer whisper,

The stars no longer gleam,

If you find yourself reaching

For a fading, distant dream,

Remember me in silence,

In the moments we did share,

In the quiet of the evening,

In the fragrance of the air.

And though I won't be with you,

In places where we used to roam,

You may not miss me; still, it can't be

Long enough till you are home.

29. Love is a Banging Parasite

It clings with silk hands, smooth as sin,

Slides into bones, burrows within.

Starts like a drug, like heaven's kiss

Then morphs into chains you never wished.

I had control -

Of my mind, my time, my goddamn soul.

Woke up with discipline, dreams in stride,

Now I wake up wondering if she lied.

Used to write poems for peace of mind,

Now every line bleeds her name inside.

Love -

You masked as light, but you're just disease.

A parasite feeding on my need to please.

You held me down with her fading scent,

And carved regret into my present tense.

Great men fell to you,

Like ancient trees with golden roots

Vincent, painting stars with madness in his head,

Shot himself still thinking of her instead.

Heathcliff, wild and strong and raw,

Turned to ruin by love's cursed law.

Napoleon, with empires in his grip,

Still haunted by Josephine's lips.

I had plans. I had fire.

Now I trade ambition for her ghost and wire.

She laughs in old messages I reread each night,

I smile at pain and call it light.

Her silence, a god I kneel before,

Hoping one more word, one more... just one more.

I tell myself it's noble,

To wait, to ache, to stay immobile.

But maybe love, like all things deep,

Needs fences too, to let us sleep.

So bang your songs, your stars, your fate

If you don't feed, don't infiltrate.

Love, if you must exist in me,

Then know this: you, too, have boundaries.

30. Surviving

When the fear of empty mornings don't let you sleep

When nightmares just haunt but don't cut you deep

When loneliness burns so much that you are drenched in sweat in a winter evening

When a full stop comes at the time of semi colon; like an abrupt ending to new beginnings

When all sorts of music once loved to sing and dance on turns into noise

When strength of confidence evaporates into invisible notes of voice

When remnants of memory defy logic and the happy moments in clouds I view

Only if this fragile life was longer, I would have embraced all the pain too.

31. Strange Adolescence

It's a strange place, this age I tread,

Where dreams run wild but peace lies dead.

Among the crowds, I walk alone,

With voices loud, yet heart like stone.

I've tried the things they said would shine,

Chased thrills and sparks that once were mine.

But joy wore off like fleeting rain,

Each new pursuit just felt the same.

Been here before, a hundred tries,

With hopeful starts and quiet goodbyes.

And still the void inside remains,

A silent ache that never wanes.

The world moves fast, I trail behind,

Their laughter stings — it's not unkind.

But something in me holds me still,

A hollow will, a restless chill.

The songs, the scenes, the days repeat,

Each echoing a slow defeat.

Where once I ran to chase the light,

Now even stars seem far from right.

I ask myself, what am I for?

A silent scream behind the door.

Will meaning come, will purpose grow,

In soils of self, I do not know?

And yet...

I dream someday, the haze will part,

A voice will speak straight to my heart.

That all I feel will find its name,

And I'll no longer feel the same.

But till that dawn, one question burns true—

"Who will answer, if not you?"

32. Resurrection

I have never been at such peace before

An absolute freedom from expectations and waiting

There is no calendar to check for happy days

For I choose to live happily every day

Neither do I check my phone the first thing after waking

Birds and breeze greet me as I meet them on the terrace

Life is accomplished happily in every way

Even if death arrives with unfulfilled goals

Thank you for making me who I am

Neither keeping my expectations in silence,

I am a small man in front of a vast ocean

The love that I gave you once I infuse into myself

There is no point in watering dead flowers

Like ventilators, keep the brain-dead alive

People pleasing is an art I no longer know

The waves come, embrace my feet, and let me go

I am the same tree that offered every fruit of mine

Never in return for a drop of water

Even when thirsty, you thrust vinegar

I am the Jesus who doesn't forgive

You may crucify my body, but not my soul.

33. Live It Slow

When I sit in silence on sunny Sundays

I feel it's heaven to where I have come

Watching sunrays route through the clouds

The beauty of the sky makes me numb.

The clock ticks and is still not looked at

As if it's attention seeking isn't working

There's more to life than live by the time

Even doing nothing seems so charming.

The world makes us feel useless as we are

When we are useful, we are used to death

Hence, we should think of ourselves too

With some love for self that arises mirth.

Live it today what has been lived unfulfilled

Since ages and stages of life so far

The childhood is gone and so is the youth

How long shall you be a collector of scars?

34. Then & Now

There's not much difference, I'd say,

Between the child I was and who I am today.

Then, too, I watched the raindrops fall,

Outside my window, gentle, small

And dreamed of days when I would be

Grown enough to taste the free:

To dance like adults in the rain,

To ride with friends down muddy lanes.

But time, that thief with quiet tread,

Gives with one hand, takes instead.

When one dream lands within your palm,

The rest dissolve, like morning calm.

And all of life begins to show,

BISMAY MOHANTY

You'll never have it all, you know.

Not at once, not all together -

Desire drifts like fickle weather.

So, I do not haunt the rooms of past,

Its echoes fade, they never last.

Nor do I chase tomorrow's haze,

A shifting path, a silent maze.

For now, is where my being stays,

The only truth that never sways.

A now I breathe, a now I give,

A now I love, a now I live.

And yes - still gazing through the pane,

I watch the dance of silver rain.

But in my eyes, no longing gleams,

For I have ceased to chase my dreams.

Not out of sorrow, nor from pain;

But peace that flows like falling rain.

35. Somebody to Love

I've wandered rooms like whispered air,
a name unsaid, a vacant stare.
Floated through days in quiet grace,
a soul with neither time nor place.

People passed through; never near,
talked around me, couldn't hear.
I laughed where silence should have been,
a ghost who learned to breathe within.

But then you turned just once, and slow,
as if you'd heard what others don't know.
Your eyes, a lantern in my mist,
a soft hello I never wished.

I felt the shape of who I am
press into light from where you stand.

The fading edges stitched anew,

just by the way you looked straight through

not past, not over, but into me,

like I was meant, like I could be.

No grand parade, no trumpet sound,

just stillness breaking sacred ground.

To be beheld, not as a prize,

but proof that I exist, alive.

And love, it wasn't stars or flight,

not thunder rolling into night

It was becoming bold and bare,

in one still moment of your care.

Now I walk and leave a trace.

My hands take shape, I claim my space.

The mirror holds a steadier view

I'm somebody, because of you.

And all the world may come or go,

but I was seen, and now I know:

To be found when you were lost above,

is the quiet miracle of somebody to love.

36. On Changes, Choices, and a Quiet Question

It doesn't shake me anymore
how the leaves fall, how they bloom,
how monsoons give way to summers,
how laughter turns into silence in a room.

The seasons come and go in their rhythm,
the people do too, in their style.
I don't flinch like I used to,
I've been still for quite a while.

The world spins,
and I spin with it—
but my center has grown quiet,
like a lamp whose flame is lit,
but doesn't leap or dance anymore.

Unfulfilled, yet whole
what a strange, sacred thing.

To not get what I wanted,

but not want what I had clung to like spring.

And when it comes to associating,

to letting someone close

my god, the cost.

The steady draining

of the energy it takes to matter

to someone who could leave,

or worse, need you back.

Maybe this is how we're trained

to hold a child one day

learning to carry

even when we're crumbling.

Learning to give

without always feeling we are living.

But deep inside the hush of my endurance

a whisper aches in the hollow:

Have I always been a burden

to the ones who dared to follow?

37. To Dissolve in the Sea

I long to be salt in the mouth of the tide,
To shed this skin where the sorrows hide,
And pour like silence into the swell,
Where time forgets, and no names dwell.

Let me be foam in the breath of the wave,
Not man nor thought, just the hush I crave,
To unmake the edges that hold me tight,
And blur into blue, beyond wrong or right.

No anchor of memory, no weight of name,
No voice to echo, no face to frame
Just the pulse of the deep, the infinite drone,
Where no one is lost, and no one's alone.

The sea does not ask where I've been,
It drinks every wound, every mortal sin.
And in its cold arms, I might forget
The sharp of regret, the sting of unmet.

So let me melt where the moonlight lies,
On the back of waves under star-stilled skies.
Let me be part of the endless sigh
Of oceans breathing, of spirits high.

To dissolve in the sea – not to die, but be
Unmade and remade in her mystery.
Not escape, but return, not flee, but find
The truth that the land had left behind.

84

More books by Bismay Mohanty:

THOUGHTS ON A TOUR

2

BISMAY MOHANTY

BISMAY MOHANTY
&
MANISH

I'M SCARED

www.ingramcontent.com/pod-product-compliance
Lightning Source LLC
Chambersburg PA
CBHW020604160726
47991CB00002B/872